RESOURCE BANK

MULTIPLICATION & DIVISION FACTS

CONTENTS

About this book

This book is designed to help Key Stage 2/P4–7 teachers and children understand multiplication and division facts and their wider application in number. Throughout the book there is an emphasis on the interrelationship of tables one to another and, using times tables as examples, explanations as to how number terms such as *multiplier, product, factor* and *prime,* arise.

The lesson plans focus on the use of the times tables and multiplication grid both of which are provided on the A1 poster. These are supported by photocopiable pages which act as supporting worksheets and provide complementary activities. After the introduction, the book is divided into two main sections.

'2–10 times tables' concentrates on reinforcing the individual times tables facts. A particular feature of the colour poster which relates to this section is the colour code. The colours are used to show how the different tables are part of a network of four basic table 'families'; a theme which is continued throughout the book.

The section 'Numbers within tables' looks at the tables through the use of the multiplication grid (also provided on the A1 poster) which is composed of products, formed by vertical and horizontal multiplier axes. The numbers which make up the basic multiplication or division 'number sentence' are interpreted in many ways: as multiples and primes; multipliers and products; dividends, divisors and quotients; numerator, denominator and whole number; factors, prime factors, powers and lowest common multiples. At the same time the inverse operations of multiplication and division, and the commutative principles of multiplication are introduced via the familiar times tables.

INTRODUCTION

About times tables

The National Curriculum, the Scottish Guidelines, DENI [Department of Education Northern Ireland] Curriculum and the Framework for Numeracy [National Numeracy Project] require that by the age of 11 all children should know the multiplication facts to 10 × 10 and should have developed mental methods for figuring out those facts they cannot instantly recall. Similarly, topics closely associated with the multiplication facts, such as patterns and properties of numbers and methods of checking results, are viewed as fundamental. (A grid showing the significance of the multiplication and division topics in this book across the curricula is given on the inside back cover of the book.)

About the poster

2–10 times tables

This side of the poster shows the times tables in a colour code. This gives an identity to each table and shows whether it is a basic table, such as 2, 3, 5 or 7, or a multiple of a basic table, such as 4 or 6 (2 × 2, and 2 × 3, respectively). Reference is made throughout the book to the colours, thus continually reinforcing the relationships between the tables. This linkage between tables can easily be lost if an ordinal order of teaching tables (2s, then 3s, then 4s, 5s and so on) is adopted.

Multiplication grid

The black and white side of the A1 poster provides a grid of the products in the times tables. The two axes can be interpreted as multipliers and can be used horizontally or vertically to find a particular number sentence. The grid has several functions. These are:

◆ To show the relationship between the three numbers which make up each number sentence in times tables. This is reinforced every time the axes are used.
◆ To introduce the commutative principle: a × b = b × a.
◆ To lead from the familiar world of the times tables towards understanding multiples, primes, fractions, factors, prime factors and lowest common multiples.
◆ To encourage the correct vocabulary for numbers for example multiplier, product, quotient.

IDEAS FOR DIFFERENTIATION

These group activities are designed to be ability differentiated. It is intended that Group A will be your less able and group C will be your more able children.

Preparing to use the poster

The poster may be most effective if it is laminated. This will then allow over-writing with whiteboard markers. It will also allow tiles (see below) to be stuck on and removed easily with tiny blobs of Blu-Tack. Three methods of hanging the poster are suggested:

◆ Holes can be punched in the corners and strengthened with reinforcement rings. It can then be pinned up.
◆ Poster hangers can be attached to the top and bottom.
◆ It can be hung up using two bulldog clips on rounded plastic sheathed hooks.

The poster should be displayed near the board, or on a flip chart, or next to a display board on which a large piece of paper can be pinned up to note the children's ideas, write up examples or demonstrate written mathematical methods.

The times tables poster is designed for close-up reference: as a long-term aide-mémoire. Encourage the children to look for features common to all the tables. However, on occasions one particular table will need to be highlighted. This can be done with a picture frame mask made from card or a folded strip of paper and held in position with Blu-tack.

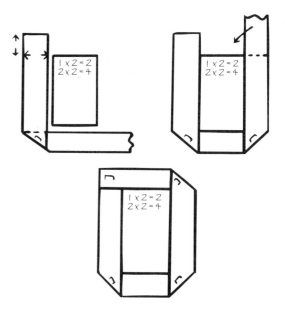

Similarly, features of the multiplication grid can be highlighted. One way is to use number markers or, for individual numbers, card tiles held on with Blu-Tack. These are simply made using white card cut into 4.5cm squares. They can be kept in a box and coloured, lettered or numbered as and when required. Attaching and removing the tiles is made easier if the poster is stiffened. You can use a backing sheet of card held with small bulldog clips if it cannot be laminated.

2–10 TIMES TABLES

This section deals individually with all the times tables from 2–10, up to 10 × 10. The '1s' times table is not shown. Encourage children to appreciate that any number multiplied by 1 remains the same.

This section develops progressively as follows:
◆ the revision of 2, 5 and 10 times tables facts, including ideas which can be applied elsewhere;
◆ a general approach to the introduction of each new table individually;
◆ the terms 'multipliers' and 'products' are introduced;
◆ table rules are suggested which offer ways of recognising patterns of some tables and how these can be used as checks in multiplication and division.

The coloured poster showing all nine tables is the focal point of this section and provides the initial impetus for most of the lessons. It can be utilised as a revision tool or as a springboard for 'puzzles' associated with multiplication and division facts.

One revision exercise that can prove particularly worthwhile is 'Today's table'. Highlight a times table with a picture frame mask (see 'Preparing to use the poster' opposite) or a simple card arrow. This can be labelled 'Today's table'. A short question and answer routine follows at some time during the day, perhaps as a prelude to a maths lesson, employing the relevant vocabulary : 'timesed by', 'multiplied by', 'how many in...'. You can also set puzzles relating to aspects of the poster which must be solved by the end of the day.

LET'S LOOK AT THE POSTER

GROUP SIZE AND ORGANISATION
Whole class.
DURATION
45–60 minutes.
LEARNING OBJECTIVE
To become familiar with the times tables poster and to appreciate the colour relationships.

YOU WILL NEED
The times tables poster, large sheet of paper pinned next to it; yellow, pink, blue and grey marker pens.

WHAT TO DO
Gather the children around the poster and ask them what the poster shows. Enquire whether they think the colours are significant or are just decorative.

Start with the 2 times table.
◆ *What colour is this table?*
◆ *Which other tables are coloured in yellow?* (4 and 8)
Count in 2s, pointing to the products (answers) column. Next do the same for 4.
◆ *What do you notice about the answers in the 2s and 4s tables?* (They are twice the size of the 2s.)
◆ *Which table has products twice the size of the 4s?* (8) *So 4 and 8 are bigger versions of the 2s.*
Next do the same for the 3 and 9 times tables.
◆ *The 9s are three times the size of the 3s. So 9 is a bigger version of 3. What other table is similar to 3? 6, but it is not red. It is orange. Look at its numbers.*
◆ *Can you see them on the 3s?* (Yes)
◆ *Can you see them anywhere else?* (The 2s column)

◆ *So 6s are made up of numbers which are in the 2 and 3 times tables.*
Using the large sheet of paper, colour in a section of it yellow. Next, shade over it in pink. The children will see that the colour changes to orange.

If the children ask about the 5 and 10 times table, use their interest to move on to the activities in 'Revising 2, 5 and 10 times tables'. If, however, you do not want to do this, move on to counting in 5s.
◆ *Where else can we see some of these numbers?* (In the tens column)
◆ *What colour are the 5s? What colour are the 10s?*
◆ *What kind of number is 10? It is an even number and the 2s numbers are yellow.*
On your sheet of paper over-colour the blue of 5 with the yellow of 2 and show how this makes the ten column green.

Recap the colours in the plenary session. Ask the children to select number sentences , such as 5 × 7 = 35, and to make up a simple story about them.

1 × 2 = 2	1 × 3 = 3	1 × 4 = 4
2 × 2 = 4	2 × 3 = 6	2 × 4 = 8
3 × 2 = 6	3 × 3 = 9	3 × 4 = 12
4 × 2 = 8	4 × 3 = 12	4 × 4 = 16
5 × 2 = 10	5 × 3 = 15	5 × 4 = 20
6 × 2 = 12	6 × 3 = 18	6 × 4 = 24
7 × 2 = 14	7 × 3 = 21	7 × 4 = 28
8 × 2 = 16	8 × 3 = 24	8 × 4 = 32
9 × 2 = 18	9 × 3 = 27	9 × 4 = 36
10 × 2 = 20	10 × 3 = 30	10 × 4 = 40
1 × 5 = 5	1 × 6 = 6	1 × 7 = 7
2 × 5 = 10	2 × 6 = 12	2 × 7 = 14
3 × 5 = 15	3 × 6 = 18	3 × 7 = 21
4 × 5 = 20	4 × 6 = 24	4 × 7 = 28
5 × 5 = 25	5 × 6 = 30	5 × 7 = 35
6 × 5 = 30	6 × 6 = 36	6 × 7 = 42
7 × 5 = 35	7 × 6 = 42	7 × 7 = 49
8 × 5 = 40	8 × 6 = 48	8 × 7 = 56
9 × 5 = 45	9 × 6 = 54	9 × 7 = 63
10 × 5 = 50	10 × 6 = 60	10 × 7 = 70
1 × 8 = 8	1 × 9 = 9	1 × 10 = 10
2 × 8 = 16	2 × 9 = 18	2 × 10 = 20
3 × 8 = 24	3 × 9 = 27	3 × 10 = 30
4 × 8 = 32	4 × 9 = 36	4 × 10 = 40
5 × 8 = 40	5 × 9 = 45	5 × 10 = 50
6 × 8 = 48	6 × 9 = 54	6 × 10 = 60
7 × 8 = 56	7 × 9 = 63	7 × 10 = 70
8 × 8 = 64	8 × 9 = 72	8 × 10 = 80
9 × 8 = 72	9 × 9 = 81	9 × 10 = 90
10 × 8 = 80	10 × 9 = 90	10 × 10 = 100

REVISING 2, 5 AND 10 TIMES TABLES

The main objectives of these activities are:
◆ to refresh table facts of the three tables;
◆ to find common links between them;
◆ to use patterns to predict beyond 10×.

COUNTING IN 2S

GROUP SIZE AND ORGANISATION
Whole class, then individuals.
DURATION
45 minutes.
LEARNING OBJECTIVES
To revise and reinforce the 2 times table. To use the patterns within the table to predict outcomes beyond 10×.

YOU WILL NEED
Times tables poster, photocopiable page 6, yellow felt-tipped pens – one per child, writing materials. For the picture frame mask – strips of paper, approximately 19cm × 27cm, stapler.

WHAT TO DO
Before the lesson highlight the 2 times table by surrounding it with a picture frame mask. (See the diagram on page 2.)

Gather the class together around the poster. Work through the 2 times table as a class, saying the table sentences and pointing to each row in turn. The table stops at 10 × 2. Explain that, using the photocopiable sheet, the children are now going to look at the times table in a different way and see if it really stops at 10, like it does on the poster.

Give each child a copy of photocopiable page 6 and a yellow felt-tipped pen and discuss counting in 2s. Starting at 2, ask the children to colour in the 2s up to 20. Explain that they can check to see if they are in the right square by referring to the times table poster. They should complete the multiplication and division table sentences on the photocopiable sheet as the squares are coloured in. When most of the class have finished, count to 10× and go over the pattern of 2.

DISCUSSION QUESTIONS
◆ *Will the pattern be the same past 20?*
◆ *Where will you colour in 11× and 12×?*
◆ *Do you think you can get to 13×? Shall we see if we can do it.*
Go over the results and then let the children work at their own speed to colour in all the twos to 100. (It is not necessary for everyone to get to 100.)

In the plenary session, gather the children around the poster with their photocopiable sheets.
◆ *Let's look at the times table poster. It ends at 10 × 2 = 20, but your 2s go on way past that. Let's count in 2s. How far can we go?*
◆ *What do all 2s end in? What other names are there for 2s?* (Pairs, twins, couples.)
◆ *Are all even numbers 2s?*
Make sure the completed photocopiable sheets are named and keep them for the next lesson.

GOING ON TO 5S

GROUP SIZE AND ORGANISATION
Whole class.
DURATION
45 minutes.
LEARNING OBJECTIVES
To revise and reinforce the 5 times table. To realise that 10× is not the end of the table. To begin to see the relationship between the 2 and 5 times tables.

YOU WILL NEED
Times tables poster, photocopiable page 6 from the previous session, light blue felt-tipped pens – one per child. For the picture frame mask – strips of paper, approximately 19cm × 27cm, stapler.

WHAT TO DO
Keep the 2 times table masked on the poster as in the previous session and put another mask around the 5s. Gather the class around the poster and work through the 5s in the same way that you did with the 2s. Tell the children that in this lesson they are going to see some maths magic happen!

Give the children their photocopiable sheets from the previous session and the light blue felt-tipped pens and ask them to colour in the 5s. As the 10s column is already shaded yellow, the children will find that these numbers will turn to green when they are coloured in. This is the 'little bit of magic'. Ask the children why they think the patterns overlapped. Draw their attention to the patterns on their sheet: the white spaces and the yellow, blue and green columns. Count in 5s. Observe how far the children can go and ask them in what numbers the 5s pattern ends.

RESOURCE BANK

MULTIPLICATION & DIVISION FACTS

REVISING 2, 5 AND 10 TIMES TABLES

During the plenary session, compare the class's findings with the poster. Have the children noticed that the 2× and 5× tables both have the tens numbers in common? *The tens column on your photocopiable sheet turned green when you coloured over it. Did you notice this was the same colour as on the times table poster? Are we likely to meet the tens again in another table?*

EXTENSION WORK
Poster Puzzle: Challenge the children to look for 2s in tables other than ×2. At the simplest level this will be 2×4, 2×5, 2×6, and so on. Later, ask them what numbers they have found. *Where are they?* Are the children aware that some numbers, such as 12, 16, 18 and 20, can be found in times tables other than ×2? Follow with 5s and 10s.

Quick Fire Counting: Carry out rapid fire counting in 2s around the class. Alternate with 'how many' questions. For instance, *How many 2s are there in 2? How many 2s in 4?* and so on. Move on to 5 and 10.

MONEY MONEY MONEY

GROUP SIZE AND ORGANISATION
At least three differentiated groups (A–C).
See 'Ideas for differentiation', page 2
DURATION
45 minutes.
LEARNING OBJECTIVE
To reinforce understanding of the 2, 5 and 10 times tables through counting coins.

YOU WILL NEED
10 coins each of 2p, 5p and 10p denominations, three different shopping items (such as a notebook, a pot, a pencil), labels marked 2p, 5p and 10p, a tray filled with a mixture of coins, three empty trays marked 2p, 5p and 10p, large sheets of paper, writing and drawing materials, times tables poster.

WHAT TO DO
The 2, 5 and 10 times tables are reflected in our coinage: 2p, 5p and 10p giving real-life examples of a set represented by a single object. For example, one 2p represents two 1p coins, and so on.

Give Group A the selection of coins and ask them to place the 2p, 5p and 10p into three individual stacks. They should then estimate what is half of each stack and divide each stack in two. Tell them to record their findings on one of the sheets of paper. (See Figure 1.)

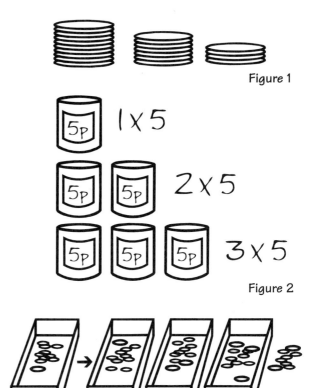

Figure 1

1 × 5

2 × 5

3 × 5

Figure 2

Figure 3

Give Group B the shopping items and ask them to choose one of the items and a price tag for it. They should then make a list for multiples of the item up to 10×. (See Figure 2.) They should then repeat this using the other two shopping items. Tell them to draw and record their findings.

Give Group C the tray filled with the mixture of coins and ask them to sort them into the three empty trays. (See Figure 3.) Ask the children how many coins there are in each tray. *What is each tray worth?* Tell the group to put a label inside each tray saying how much it contains. They should draw and record their findings.

During the plenary session, discuss each group's work and their findings. Leave their work on display.

ASSESSMENT
Are the children counting in steps and using multiplication facts to record the number and value of the coins? Discourage repeated 'tag' counting of coins; for example, touching each 2p twice while saying, 'One, two...three, four... five, six...' and so on.

EXTENSION WORK
Mental Maths: use 10p coins to revise the 2, 5 and 10 times tables: *Show me 20p in 10s. How many 5s? How many 2s? How many 10s in 50p? How many 5s? Let's make the tables into pence tables. If we put 'p' where would it go? Say the tables as pence tables: 1 × 2p = 2p.*

TABLES REVISION

Name _____   Date _____

1	2	3	4	5	6	7	8	9	10
11	12	13	14	15	16	17	18	19	20
21	22	23	24	25	26	27	28	29	30
31	32	33	34	35	36	37	38	39	40
41	42	43	44	45	46	47	48	49	50
51	52	53	54	55	56	57	58	59	60
61	62	63	64	65	66	67	68	69	70
71	72	73	74	75	76	77	78	79	80
81	82	83	84	85	86	87	88	89	90
91	92	93	94	95	96	97	98	99	100

1 × ☐ = ☐   ☐ ÷ ☐ = 1
2 × ☐ = ☐   ☐ ÷ ☐ = 2
3 × ☐ = ☐   ☐ ÷ ☐ = 3
4 × ☐ = ☐   ☐ ÷ ☐ = 4
5 × ☐ = ☐   ☐ ÷ ☐ = 5
6 × ☐ = ☐   ☐ ÷ ☐ = 6
7 × ☐ = ☐   ☐ ÷ ☐ = 7
8 × ☐ = ☐   ☐ ÷ ☐ = 8
9 × ☐ = ☐   ☐ ÷ ☐ = 9
10 × ☐ = ☐   ☐ ÷ ☐ = 10

PREDICTIONS

11 × ☐ = ☐   ☐ ÷ ☐ = 11
12 × ☐ = ☐   ☐ ÷ ☐ = 12
13 × ☐ = ☐   ☐ ÷ ☐ = 13
14 × ☐ = ☐   ☐ ÷ ☐ = 14
15 × ☐ = ☐   ☐ ÷ ☐ = 15

MULTIPLICATION AND DIVISION FACTS

INDIVIDUAL TABLES

The following is a model lesson which can be adapted for use either to introduce any times table or to be taught alongside any table in its introductory phase.

COUNTING IN

GROUP SIZE AND ORGANISATION
Whole class.
DURATION
45 minutes.
LEARNING OBJECTIVES
To identify the unique times table pattern by counting and colouring in each product. To predict multiplication facts beyond ×10.

YOU WILL NEED
Times tables poster, fresh copies of photocopiable page 6, felt-tipped pens to match the colour code of whichever times table you are studying, writing materials.

WHAT TO DO
This activity looks at multiplication up to 10. The next activity extends this learning so that the children become confident with the knowledge that multiplication is not something that ceases at 10 but can be continued indefinitely.

Draw the class's attention to the poster and identify the times table you are going to study. For example, if you are going to study 4:
◆ *Today we are going to look at the 4 times table. Can you show me where this is on the poster?*
◆ *What are its numbers?*
◆ *Where else is the table?* If the children have already identified the complete vertical layout, see if they can find the ×4 horizontal sentences in each of the other tables. (This is the fourth horizontal multiplication line in each table.)

◆ *When you are working, you will be looking for these numbers in a different way.*
Remind the children that they can look at the poster whenever they want to check what they are doing.

Hand each child a copy of photocopiable page 6 and explain to them how to count along and colour the squares of the 100 square, for example if you are studying the 4 times table, it would be: *1, 2, 3, colour in 4 in yellow.* Make sure the pupils understand the wrap-round at the end of each row:
◆ *When we get to 10, where is the next number?* Emphasise to the class that in this lesson you only want them to shade in the table up to 10×. Go round the class, checking that the children are confident about what they are doing. Then direct the children to the number sentences below the 100 square.
◆ *What two number sentences go with 1×?* ($1 \times 4 = 4$; $4 \div 4 = 1$)
As each square is coloured in, encourage the children to complete the multiplication and division number sentences underneath the 100 square.

Discuss the pattern made by the table. Keep the photocopiables for use in the next lesson. Pose the children a cliff-hanger for the next session. Point to the times table poster and ask:
◆ *If we wanted to go further than 10× to 11× where would we go? We will talk about this next time.*

IDEAS FOR DISPLAY
Make a 'train' to show the ordinal order of a specific table in conjunction with its products. Create a tables locomotive and attach 'product' wagons behind it in an ordinal order. If you want to use it repeatedly make it out of cards and laminate them. Depending on which table you are focusing on, numbers and dots can then be written on using a washable marker pen. The cards are easily stored in a box. The children can also create a 'makes what' box car. This can be a variation of 'Today's Table' and the children can make a different length of train each day. It can be used as a desktop aid for any child with learning difficulties.

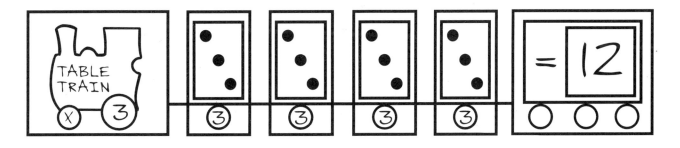

INDIVIDUAL TABLES

COUNTING ON

GROUP SIZE AND ORGANISATION
Whole class.
DURATION
45 minutes.
LEARNING OBJECTIVE
To learn that multiplication patterns can be predicted beyond ×10.

YOU WILL NEED
Times tables poster, photocopiable page 6 from the previous lesson, writing and drawing materials.

WHAT TO DO
Give the children back their photocopiable sheets from the previous session and recap with them how they got to 10 × 4.
◆ *Can we find 11×?*
Use the same counting technique as in the previous lesson, but tell the children that this time you would like them to fill in the prediction boxes.
◆ *What number did we finish on in the last lesson? (40: 10 × 4)*
◆ *Now can we complete the 11× number sentence?*
◆ *What other sentence goes with 11? (44 ÷ 4 = 11) Do this one as well.*
Go round the class supervising. If the children are confident with what they are doing, let them complete the prediction boxes to 15×. (Note that, depending on which table you are studying, products may become larger than 100. In these cases the children will have to work them out mentally.)

As a table is completed, the pattern of its numbers and its predictability should be emphasised. Children can describe the pattern of the columns or diagonals.

IDEAS FOR DISPLAY
A card strip frieze marked 1–100 and pinned around the room is invaluable. When a table is being introduced, attach paper-clips to the frieze to show 'jumps' along the number line. Use coloured paper-clips in the corresponding times tables colours (yellow for 2s, and so on). Write down the ordinal order of the table on cards and attach these to the 'jumps' along the number line, thus defining each position in the times table. So, for example, if you are studying the 2 times table you would attach cards marked 'first', 'second', 'third' to the multiples of 2: 2, 4, 6, and so on.

TABLES MODELS

GROUP SIZE AND ORGANISATION
Three differentiated groups (A–C).
DURATION
30 minutes.
LEARNING OBJECTIVE
To extend understanding of multiplication.

YOU WILL NEED
55 bricks or cubes, thin card (some of it large enough to draw around a plate), different-coloured paper or card the width of a metre ruler, coins, a metre stick, Blu-Tack, scissors, drawing materials, a plate.

WHAT TO DO
In these differentiated group activities, the children explore mathematical models of tables: a grid, a 'real' number line and product sets.

Group A – Blocks Staircase: Give Group A the bricks or cubes, some thin card, scissors and some drawing materials. Tell the children to draw around one face of a brick onto the thin card and then cut it out.

Depending on which table number you are studying, the children should then draw the appropriate number of dots on to the card. Using small blobs of Blu-Tack, they should then stick the card onto the brick. (If you are studying a times table beyond six, then the children will need two pieces of card as they will be using two faces of the brick, 6 +1, +2, and so on.)

The children then build an ascending staircase from 1 to 10. Discuss how many bricks there are in each column, the total of the column and the fact that the rows across are the same as the columns.
◆ *Show me three sevens across.*
◆ *Is there another way of showing three sevens?*
◆ *What do three sevens equal?*

Group B – Metre Stick: Give this group the metre ruler, the different-coloured paper or card, scissors and some Blu-Tack. Explain that you would like the children to measure and then cut out ten sections the same length

RESOURCE
BANK

MULTIPLICATION & DIVISION FACTS

INDIVIDUAL TABLES

as the assigned times table you are studying so, for instance, if you are studying the 7× table the sections should be 7 cm long. Each section should be in a different colour. The sections are then stuck onto the blank side of the ruler using small blobs of Blu-Tack. No two colours should adjoin. Focus discussion on various aspects of the table. For instance:

◆ *What do three sections add up to?*
◆ *How many sections fit into half a metre?*
◆ *Do they fit exactly or is there something left over?*

Group C – Coin Sets: Give this group some pieces of card, a plate to cut around, some scissors, drawing materials, the coins and some Blu-Tack. Tell the children to draw round the plate on the card and cut out ten circles. The assigned times table number is then made up using an assortment of coins, each plate representing a stage in the table. So, for instance, if you are studying 3s, the first circle could contain a 2p and 1p, the second circle could show 6p using a 5p and a 1p, and 9p could be shown by two 2p pieces and a 5p. When all the combinations have been covered, tell the children to repeat.

Discuss the results with the children during a plenary session.

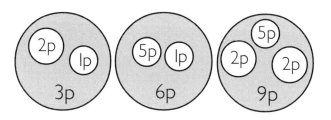

IDEAS FOR DISPLAY
Leave the 'models' on a display table for children to handle and see for themselves.

EXTENSION WORK
Poster Puzzle: early in the day, spend 10 minutes setting the class the task of discovering in what tables are the same products (answers) as the assigned table. For example, if the 7× table is being studied, ask the children where else they can find the same products as in 7x. Towards the end of the day, spend another ten minutes asking the class for examples. As they give answers, ask the rest of the class to assess whether they are correct. Give each child a card with a tick on one side and a cross on the other: *Is Anna's answer right or wrong? Hold up your cards now.* By using this method, you have an instant way of assessing the general ability of the class as each child is not given the chance to copy anyone else's answer.

WORRY BEADS

GROUP SIZE AND ORGANISATION
Pairs or individuals.
DURATION
Three sessions of 20 minutes each.
LEARNING OBJECTIVE
To make and use a resource, 'worry beads', to reinforce multiplication facts.

YOU WILL NEED
Session one: for each set of beads 10 strips of sugar paper $2\frac{1}{2}$ cm wide by 20 cm long, adhesive.
Session two: times table poster, paints corresponding to the colours on the poster, dried paper tubes.
Session three: painted beads, string or strong coloured thread (about $\frac{1}{2}$ metre long) one per child, lots of small sticky labels and pens.

WHAT TO DO
Worry beads allow children who are unsure of tables a chance to combine counting with a tactile action; passing the beads through their fingers. This would be an ideal craft activity to carry out when all the times tables have been completed. For these sessions, the class is split into pairs with each pair assigned to a different table from 2–10. (In a class with over 18 children, some tables will be repeated.) The beads can be kept hanging from hooks to be used when needed.
Session one. Give each child a strip of sugar paper and tell them to write their name on one side and then paste the other side. The strip is then wound tightly round a pencil. Lay them on newspaper to dry.
Session two. Allot a times table to each child or pair. Tell them to collect their dried paper tube and then to colour it in the correct colour code, yellow for 2s, pink for 3s, and so on. They can refer to the poster if necessary. When this has been done, lay them on newspaper to dry.
Session three. Give each child or pair some labels, pens or pencils and lengths of thread. Tell them to colour the background of the label the same colour as the bead. If two children are working together, one child writes the numbers of the times table in ascending order on his or her label while the other child draws dots to represent that table. The label should then be stuck on the sugar paper. Thread the beads on the string and tie a knot. Once the strings of beads are completed, demonstrate how they can be moved through the fingers while saying '5, 10, 15, 20...' or 'One 2 is two', two 2s are 4...'.

MULTIPLIERS AND PRODUCTS

The terms 'multiplicand', 'multiplier' and 'product' are introduced in relation to tables number sentences.

M × M = P

GROUP SIZE AND ORGANISATION
Whole class.
DURATION
60 minutes.
LEARNING OBJECTIVE
To learn the terms 'multiplicand', 'multiplier' and 'product' in relation to each other.

YOU WILL NEED
Sheet of paper, thin stiff card, card, scissors, adhesive, small box, large empty matchbox, crumpled paper, large cube, felt-tipped pens or paints the same colours as the times tables poster, plant pot, 'right, wrong' cards as used in 'Tables models', times tables poster.

WHAT TO DO
Draw a circle approximately 20 cm in diameter on the sheet of paper. Divide the card into ten even sections and write the number of the times table in each of the sections beginning with 1 × .

Cut out the circle and attach it to the centre of a piece of thin card. On the back of the card attach a small box about the size of a large matchbox. Stuff this with the crumpled paper to give it stability. Attach the box to another piece of card. Make two holes in this backing piece of card so that it can be pinned up. A large coloured paper-clip can be used as a pointer to whichever table is being studied.

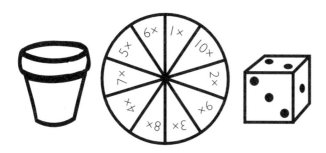

Next make a monster dice using a large cube. Colour the six sides the same colour as the poster code: yellow, pink, blue, grey, orange and green. Then draw on the dots 1–6. Use a plant pot as a shaker for the dice. The children will also need right or wrong cards.

Pin up the times table poster and the wheel in a prominent position. Place the monster dice and the plant pot on a low table. Split the class into nine groups each representing a table from 2–10.

Talk about a table number sentence. Explain or remind the children that a number sentence tells us a story about things happening to numbers.
- *How do we write '8 times (or multiplies) 7 makes (equals) 56?'* (Write this on the board.)
- *What number started the whole thing? 8, 7 or 56?* (8)
- *8 is the 'how many number'. It tells us how many sets of a number, but this is not the starter number. It is the multiplier.*
- *What about 56? No. It is at the end of the operation. Things have had to happen before 56 was made.*
- *Has anyone ever been to a factory? What is made in a factory?* (Products) *So we could say 56 has been made by our number factory and so it is the product.*
- *Now all we have left is 7. This is the starter number, the number to which everything happens. This is called an unusual name, the multiplicand.* (You may need to explain a discrepancy here between spoken and mathematical convention. In language we would tend to refer to eight groups (times) of seven with the multiplicand second. However, in written form, when the multiplicand is more than ten, we usually put it first, for instance as 23 × 6 (6 sets of 23). Experience will show the children which is which.
- *There are three numbers in our multiplication sentences: the starter number or multiplicand; the sets of number or multiplier; and the number made by the other two numbers or the product.*

Draw examples from each times table, identifying the multiplicand, the multiplier and the product.

Now play the game. Shake the dice in the plant pot, throw it and look at the number and colour that is shown. Using the paper-clip count around the wheel from 1. The number you stop on becomes the multiplier. (The next throw of the dice carries it on from here.) Next look at the colour. This tells you the multiplicand. If it is orange, blue, grey or green then only one table will apply. Ask the appropriate times table group what product the wheel multiplier gives when multiplying their table. If the colour is yellow or pink, then each of the different groups with different multiplicands have to give their 'answers'.

ASSESSMENT
In your plenary session hold a question and answer session without using any of the games props.
6 multiplied by 9: What is the product? 54. *What is the multiplier?* 6. *So what does the sentence say? There are 6 sets or groups of 9. What else could it mean? There are 9 sets of 6. Does the product change in this case?*

RESOURCE BANK

MULTIPLICATION & DIVISION FACTS

MULTIPLIERS AND PRODUCTS

EXTENSION WORK

Poster puzzle: on a succession of days set a task in the morning from the times tables poster to be completed by the afternoon:

◆ *Find the 5 smallest products. What multiplicands and multipliers make them?*
◆ *Find the 5 biggest products. What multiplicands and multipliers make them?*
◆ *Find all the odd products up to 49.*
◆ *Find all the even products to 50.*
◆ *Find all the odd products to 99.*
◆ *Find all the even products to 100.*

INSIDE THE SHAPES

GROUP SIZE AND ORGANISATION
Whole class then pairs.
DURATION
45 minutes.
LEARNING OBJECTIVE
To relate, then reinforce, the parts of a multiplication sentence.

YOU WILL NEED

Times tables poster, a large quantity of A4 scrap paper cut into quarter page strips.

WHAT TO DO

Revise the previous lesson by looking at the times tables poster with the class. Discuss what a product is. Show the class the products in the 7 times table. Then look at another table:

◆ *Now what about the multipliers. Someone show me the multipliers column in the 8s table.*
◆ *So on our tables the multipliers are shown first. This leaves one other number in each number sentence which we have not named. Which one is it?*
◆ *Show me in the 2s table? 3s? This is the multiplicand.* (Pick a number sentence from the poster.) *Now let's see what each number is called.*

Organise the class into pairs. (There is no need to

worry about ability grouping as each pair will work to their own ability.) Recap the three names of a table number sentence. Explain that, using the strips of paper, you would like the children to make some table sentences of their own but you would like them to show these in a different way. On the strips of paper they should draw a triangle, a multiplication sign, a circle, an equal sign and a square. They should write the multiplicand inside the triangle and the multiplier inside the circle. The square will show the product. Write an example on the board as you explain it.

Give the class time to absorb this information and then get started. Go round helping and advising. Remind the class that they can check their work against the poster if they need confirmation of any number.

IDEAS FOR DISPLAY

As the strips are completed, ask the children to bring them to you to check that they are correct. They can then be pinned up to create an instant wall display. Sit the class facing the display. Go over the examples, including one at least from every pair.

EXTENSION WORK

Spare time activity cards: the elements of the multiplication sentence can be made into a spare time activity card game. Create some circular, triangular and square shapes on pieces of thin card. Draw round these and create ten copies of each shape. Write the numbers 1–10 on the circular and triangular cards. Choose a times table and write the product of this table on the square cards. On a piece of thin but stiff card cut out circular, triangular and square shapes into which the cards will fit. On the card, using a thick felt-tipped pen, draw in the multiplication and equal signs. Hand out the cards to the players. Tell them to shuffle the cards face down. One of the circles is then turned over and put in its place on the board. A triangle is then picked out. This sets the puzzle for the right product. Each player then turns over the squares until the winner finds the right product. If it is not the correct answer the card is replaced. (If you wish to make the game more complicated, tell the children to shuffle the cards around after each choice.)

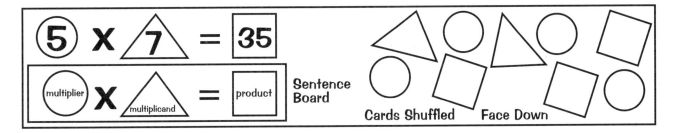

TABLE RULES

READ THE RULES

GROUP SIZE AND ORGANISATION
Whole class then individuals.
DURATION
60 minutes.
LEARNING OBJECTIVES
To see how patterns in the times tables lead to methods of checking multiplication and division operations. To encourage checking for 'reasonableness' in answers.

YOU WILL NEED
Photocopiable page 14 (guillotine this in half and retain the lower part of the sheet 'Fishing' for a later activity), right/wrong cards (see 'Tables models'), writing and drawing materials (the colours should correspond to the poster), times tables poster, Blu-Tack, nine sheets of dark paper, approximately 14cm x 27cm.

WHAT TO DO
NB. The rules for this activity are based on the premise that the digits within an 'answer' can be used in some way to check whether that answer fits within a particular table. 2, 3, 5, 9 and 10 tables have such rules. 7 does not. 4 and 8 fit the 2s rule but there is no way of differentiating them from 2s. Only every other even number is divisible by 4. 32 is, 34 is not, while only one even number in four is divisible by 8.

Using the dark sheets of paper, cover all the times tables except for the products columns.
◆ *Look at the products.*
◆ *How can we tell what tables they belong to?* (The position and colour are the obvious answers.)
◆ *What else?* (By now the children should be looking at the type of number: 2s numbers are all evens; 5s numbers have a pattern of 5 and 0; 10s all end in noughts.)
◆ *What about 3s?*
◆ *Add the digits in each product line.* (12 is 1 + 2 which makes 3, 15 is 1 + 5 which makes 6, and so on.) *All the numbers are 3s. Let's try the rest of the 3s family. Count across the products of 9 and they all become 9s. Do the same for 6. They do not add up to 6 but they do follow the 3s rule and the 2s rule.*

Give out copies of the top half of photocopiable page 14. Instruct the class to fold the sheet in half with the 'Rules' inside. Explain that you would like them to write their name and draw a design for the outside

cover. They should then colour the number logos in the corresponding poster colour codes.

Explain to the children how they can use a checking device. This can be used after multiplication to see that the product they have gained is correct or nearabouts. While it will not prove the 'answer' is right, it could prove it was wrong.
◆ *Suppose I got 97 as the product of 23 × 3, is my answer on the right lines?*
◆ *Apply the rule. So for 3s we would add the digits in the product line. In this instance they come to 16.*
◆ *Does this divide by 3 exactly? No, so my answer is wrong and I should try again.*

The rules work even better for division. If the rules are used before dividing, it is possible to see whether a number can be divided exactly or not. Again the rule does not give the 'answer', but it does show if it is wrong.
◆ *Is 5678 divisible by 9? Why not?* (Because all the digits do not add to a number that can be divided by 9 exactly.)

Hand out the right/wrong cards and work through the rules using various examples. Tell the children to hold up their cards when they've checked the answer.
◆ *25 multiplied by 5 possibly makes 127? Right or wrong?*
◆ *36 multiplied by 3 possibly makes 108? Right or wrong?*
◆ *Does 3 go into 596 exactly?*
◆ *Does 9 go into 987 exactly? Does 6? Does 3?*
Write on the board a number with as many digits as you like but end it with 0.
◆ *Does 5 go into it? Does 10 go into it?*

ASSESSMENT
Ask individual children to think of three figure numbers which can be divided by 2, 3, and so on. Again the rest of the class should use their right/wrong cards to say whether or not they think these answers are correct.

IDEAS FOR DISPLAY
Ask the children to design reminder posters explaining these rules and how they help us check the answers.

TABLE RULES

IS IT DIVISIBLE?

GROUP SIZE AND ORGANISATION
Class divided into six groups.
DURATION
30 minutes.
LEARNING OBJECTIVE
To check numbers to see if they divide exactly into one or other of the six tables.

YOU WILL NEED
Children's completed 'books' from the previous session, right/wrong cards, chalkboard/flip chart.

WHAT TO DO
Organise the class into six groups, each representing one of the tables (2, 3, 5, 6, 9, 10). Write the following list of numbers on the board: 96, 78, 125, 468, 890, 709, 517. Tell the children they are going to find which tables divide into these numbers exactly. Begin with 96. Consult the tables groups in turn starting with 2s.
◆ *Does 2 go into it? (Yes.) Why? Write × 2 after 96.* Consult the 3s group.
◆ *Does 3 go into it? (Yes.) Why? Write × 3 after the × 2.* Consult the 5s group.
◆ *Does 5 go into it? (No.) Why not? Do not write anything after the × 3.*
Carry on with the other groups. Then ask the different groups to go through the rest of the numbers noting those which are divisible by their particular table.

In the plenary session, go through each number, asking each group's opinion and writing the results alongside each number.
◆ *Which number was divisible by the most tables? Which number was divisible by the least?*

FISHING

GROUP SIZE AND ORGANISATION
Whole class then individuals then whole class.
DURATION
30 minutes.
LEARNING OBJECTIVE
To practise using the quick check rules.

YOU WILL NEED
Photocopiable page 14 (you will need the bottom half

of the sheet for this activity), felt-tipped pens the same colours as on the poster, times tables poster, A5 size card, six plastic trays, coloured card.

WHAT TO DO
Gather the class around the poster. Go through the six tables (2, 3, 5, 6, 9, 10) and their colours. Give each child a copy of the bottom half of photocopiable page 14. Explain to the children that they are going to be fishermen catching different fish. When they 'catch' one, they must shade it in according to the colour of the table which divides into its number. So, for instance, if the fish marked number 39 is caught, ask the children what they would colour it? (Pink because it is divisible by 3.) Once a fish has been 'caught' the children must not 'catch' it again.

When the sheets are completed, bring the class together and look at the colours the children have used. If the same fish has been shaded differently by some children, discuss why this may have been done. Is the number the product of more than one table?

EXTENSION ACTIVITY
Split the class into six groups and assign each group to one of the six tables. Hand out the A5 card and explain that each child must draw a fish on one side of the card (this can be any type: shellfish, octopus, shark, goldfish, and so on). When they have done this they should colour it in using the felt-tipped pens. It does not have to conform to the colour code of their table. On the reverse, each child should write any number over 100 which is divisible by their group's times table.

While the children are doing this, write the number of each of the tables (2, 3, 5, 6, 9, 10) on the pieces of coloured card. Attach these to the front of the trays. Ask the children to spread their cards face down. Players turn over a 'fish' and choose which 'boat' to put it in. The onlookers decide if the choice is correct.

ASSESSMENT
The children should give reasons for their choice of boat based on the tables 'rules' or tables facts that they can recall.

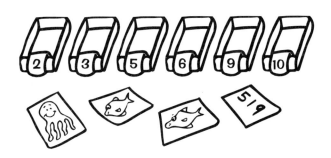

TABLE RULES

QUICK CHECK RULES

 Last digit must be even – 4 6 8 0

 Last digit must be even and all digits must add to a number that divides by 3 exactly.

 All digits must add to a number that divides by 3 exactly.

 All digits must add to a number that divides by 9 exactly.

 Last digit must be 5 or 0.

 Last digit must be 0.

26	39	44	65	78	91	98
540	117	235	816	457	704	822
505	830	56	519	700	51	350
3080	2184	1967	8112	3285	2991	9657
44984	31197	60184	197676	76044	89617	21789

MULTIPLICATION AND DIVISION FACTS

NUMBERS WITHIN TABLES

This section of the book is concerned with the characteristics of the products of the tables 2–10. New terms relating to number properties are introduced which go beyond times tables, but which use the familiar world of the times tables to facilitate understanding of them.

In this part of the book, the sections are linked. Tables Families is followed by Multiples and Primes. Multiplication and Division go with Fractions. The Commutative Calculator precedes Factors Tables which rework the same concept. Prime Factor Trees and Powers and Lowest Common Multiples round off 'table families', 'multiples', 'factors' and 'primes' in an all embracing mathematical operation.

The topics covered are:
◆ multiples of the basic four times table 'families' under 10 in which the colour code on the poster plays an interactive part;
◆ multiples and primes, where the basic tables are used to discover all the primes in the 100 square;
◆ multiplication and division as inverse operations;
◆ fractions expressed as division sentences;
◆ commutative calculations, expressed algebraically as: $a \times b = b \times a = c$;

◆ factors tables, where 'multipliers' are seen as pairs of numbers making a product;
◆ prime factors of numbers are discovered via a factor 'tree' which refers back to the basic four tables;
◆ multiplication trains are shortened to powers and from these and prime factors lowest common multiples are identified.

The black and white multiplication grid poster provided with this book shows the relationship between the three numbers in a multiplication sentence.

By giving the two axes equal weighting, the commutative principles of $a \times b = b \times a$ are overtly suggested. This is underlined by the inclusion of '1' as a multiplier. Throughout this section the three numbers are reinterpreted largely through the poster and trios of tiles.

The introductory poster session before each main class lesson is seen as a way of revising a previous concept while paving the way to introduce a new one. Similarly the use of blank tiles suggested in many of the activities forces the child to think about the hidden numbers.

LET'S LOOK AT THE POSTER

GROUP SIZE AND ORGANISATION
Whole class.
DURATION
30 minutes.
LEARNING OBJECTIVE
To learn how the grid is used and how the three sets of numbers on it interact.

YOU WILL NEED
The multiplication grid side of the poster, two card strips, one the width of the poster, the other the length of it – both to be kept near the poster, Blu-Tack.

WHAT TO DO
Make sure that the children are sitting so that they are all able to see the poster clearly. Ask them:
◆ *What have we got on the poster?*
(Hopefully, they will be able to tell you that it shows

the multiplication facts/times tables written across and down.)
◆ *It is a grid which is a bit like a crossword puzzle. To make sense of it, you have to look at it across and down. If I want to find '6 × 9', then I look along the 6s like this* (use the width strip) *and put another strip down alongside which number?* (The first child to answer 9 can stick the long strip in place.) *Now let's make up some multiplier number sentences and see if you can find them.*

Allow two children at a time to come out and hold the strips while the rest of the class give examples.

IDEAS FOR DISPLAY
The multipliers identification bars on the top and left-hand side of the poster can be coloured in to give them more prominence. They should be: 1 white (left uncoloured); 2, 4 and 8 in yellow; 3 and 9 in pink; 5 in blue; 6 in orange; 7 in grey and 10 in green.

A copy of the poster grid is given on photocopiable page 18. This can be pinned up next to the poster and coloured in the same colours as above. However, this should not be introduced until the Table Families section has been completed.

FAMILY LIKENESS

GROUP SIZE AND ORGANISATION
Whole class.
DURATION
60 minutes.
LEARNING OBJECTIVE
To discover/reinforce that some times tables
are multiples of the four basic tables
'families' (2, 3, 5, 7).

YOU WILL NEED
Poster; photocopiable page 18 (plus an enlarged copy
for demonstration with the class), yellow, pink, blue and
grey felt-tipped pens, thin card, paste, Blu-Tack
(optional).

WHAT TO DO
(The photocopiable sheet required for this activity
needs to be pasted onto card and left to dry. This
activity, therefore, may best be done as a short 'fill-in'
lesson when paste has been used for some other
project.)

Show the class the times table side of the poster
and ask if they remember the colours. *Why do you think
they were chosen?* Tell them that in this lesson they will
be finding out the answer to this. Explain that the
photocopiable sheet they will be using has a copy of
the multiplication grid on it like the one on the poster.

Using your enlarged copy of photocopiable page 18,
demonstrate to the children what you would like them
to do. Colour the vertical 2s column in yellow (or use
yellow card tiles which you can attach to the grid
poster with Blu-Tack). Give each child a copy of
photocopiable page 18 and tell them that they will be
completing this sheet.

Ask the children what the next 2s table is. Elicit
from the class that the 4 times table is in fact another
variation of the 2s as it has the same numbers in it,
only doubled, so the 4s should be yellow. Ask the
children what other tables are even numbers, thus
making them part of the 2s family. Hopefully, the
children will say 6, 8 and 10. Explain that we therefore
now have five yellow columns showing all the tables in
the 2s family.

Next, using the pink felt-tipped pen, work through
the same procedure for 3s. The next 3s number is 6 so
the children should colour over the yellow of the 2s.
When they have done this, ask them what has

happened and why. Again, make sure the children
understand that 6 is part of the 2s and the 3s families.
Move onto 9. *Is this already coloured? No. Colour it in.*
Do the children see that 6 and 9 are part of the 3s
family? Remind the class that the orange is comprised
of the yellow of 2 and the pink of 3. (The colour link is
not merely what the children can see now but what
they have observed. They know they have coloured 6
in pink as part of the 3s. The mixture gives orange
made up of the yellow and the pink, just as 6, 12, 18,
24 and any multiple of 6 is comprised of 2 and 3.)

Next the children should colour in the 5s column in
blue. Do the children notice that the colour of the
tens column changes when they colour over it? This is
because 10 was already coloured in yellow because it
belongs to the 2s family. Move onto 7. Colour it grey. It
has no multiples below 10.

Ask the children if they can now see why the times
tables poster was coloured in the way it was. It shows
the different families of tables. Recap with the class. The
2s family is coloured in yellow. The 3s family is
coloured in pink. 6 is in orange because it belongs to
both family tables. The 5s family is coloured in blue. 10
is in green because it belongs to the 5s and the 2s
families. The 7s family is in grey — it has no other tables
family under 10. Tell the children to write their names
on the photocopiable sheet and store them for the
next lesson.

IDEAS FOR DISPLAY
Leave four completed copies of the photocopiable
sheet on display alongside the poster, showing the
different families.

TABLE FAMILIES

MAKE A CALCULATOR

GROUP SIZE AND ORGANISATION
Individuals then whole class.
DURATION
45 minutes.
LEARNING OBJECTIVE
To reinforce and practise using the relationship between multipliers and product.

YOU WILL NEED
Completed photocopiable sheets from previous session, two strips of thin, flexible card per child 40cm × 1.5cm, scissors, sticky tape or adhesive.

WHAT TO DO
Hand each child the strips of card, scissors and adhesive and their completed photocopiable sheets from the previous lesson. Tell them to follow the instructions given to make the calculator strips. Explain that these will be used to fit over the photocopiable grid which they completed in the previous session. (They will need to cut out their multiplication grid.)

When the children have completed making their grids, practise using them as calculators. (Make sure the children can all move the strips across their grids to highlight the answer.) Ask the class for two numbers between 1 and 10. *What is their product?*
Reverse the exercise and have the product first.
- *What are the two multipliers?*
- *What families are the multipliers in?*
- *Does any product appear more than once? With the same multipliers?*

WORK IT OUT!

GROUP SIZE AND ORGANISATION
Whole class.
DURATION
30 minutes looking at the poster then daily 10 minute lesson.
LEARNING OBJECTIVE
To explore the multiplication patterns in the grid.

YOU WILL NEED
Blank 4.5cm paper tiles placed in a box underneath the poster, small blobs of Blu-Tack, multiplication grid poster.

WHAT TO DO
Gather the class around the multiplication grid poster and demonstrate how a number sequence goes horizontally across each table, for example the 2s are 2, 4, 6, 8, 10, 12, and so on. Explain that if a number is covered up then this hidden number can be worked out if the rest of the table is known. Ask the class to close their eyes and then stick one of the paper tiles over the number 6. Tell the class to open their eyes and ask them what the missing number is. Reiterate that, although the sequence is broken, the missing number can be worked out from the number before and the number after. Continue playing the game, but allow different children to cover over the numbers.

IDEAS FOR DISPLAY
The children could colour in four photocopiables to display beside the grid, each as a different family: 2s, 4s, 6s, 8s, 10s in yellow; 3s, 6s, 9s in pink; 5s and 10s in blue and 7s in grey.

EXTENSION WORK
Poster puzzle: stick blank squares on the poster every day and ask the children to find the missing numbers. Move on to using three or four squares. Go over the sequences later in the day.

TABLE FAMILIES

Name _____   Date _____

X	1	2	3	4	5	6	7	8	9	10
1	1	2	3	4	5	6	7	8	9	10
2	2	4	6	8	10	12	14	16	18	20
3	3	6	9	12	15	18	21	24	27	30
4	4	8	12	16	20	24	28	32	36	40
5	5	10	15	20	25	30	35	40	45	50
6	6	12	18	24	30	36	42	48	54	60
7	7	14	21	28	35	42	49	56	63	70
8	8	16	24	32	40	48	56	64	72	80
9	9	18	27	36	45	54	63	72	81	90
10	10	20	30	40	50	60	70	80	90	100

✂ -

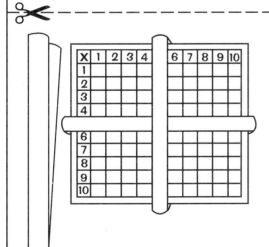

To make a calculator.

You will need two strips of card 40cm × 1.5cm.

Fold them in half.
Place them across and down the calculator.
Stick the ends with sticky tape or adhesive.
Leave a tab at the end to use as a handle.

PHOTOCOPIABLE
RESOURCE
BANK

MULTIPLES AND PRIMES

In this section, children discover multiples and primes between 1 and 100 using the basic four table families. They use the words 'multiple' and 'prime'. 'Common multiple' is introduced.

PRIME SIEVE

GROUP SIZE AND ORGANISATION
Whole class then individuals.
DURATION
60 minutes.
LEARNING OBJECTIVE
To find the 'primes' in the 100 square by eliminating the 'multiples'.

YOU WILL NEED
100 square grid – one per child (you could use the 100 square on photocopiable page 6, you may like to enlarge this), multiplication grid poster, tiles with 'm-m' on them, Blu-tack, 18 'm' tiles, some 'cm' tiles.

WHAT TO DO
Give each child a copy of the 100 square then tell the class to gather around the multiplication grid poster. Focus their attention on the poster and point out the first row across. Count the numbers 1, 2, 3, 4, 5, and so on up to 10. Examine how the next row starts with 2, 4, 6. Ask how that is different to a 100 square. Tell the children to look at their 100 squares. Point out that the second row starts with 11. Continue counting across that row. Refer the children back to the multiplication grid and explain that this is not the same as the 100 square. *Are there any numbers missing?* Examples could be 11, 13, 17, or any other prime number. Explain to the children that these are special numbers which they are going to find out more about. Ask them to return to their seats and tell them the story below.

Eratosthenes was a Greek mathematician who lived 2000 years ago. He imagined a huge sieve or net which caught all the numbers in the times tables but which let free all the other numbers. The numbers he caught were multiples and the ones left free were primes. So that he knew which was which he crossed out all the numbers which are made by multiplying other numbers. We call these 'multiples'.

The following question and answer procedure can be followed for each successive table.

◆ *Start at 2. Is 2 a multiple? Is it made by two other*

numbers? 1 × 2, but all numbers can be multiplied by 1 so 2 is not a multiple. It is not struck out.

◆ *Count/add on 2. Is 4 a multiple? It is a 'made' number because 2 × 2 makes 4. Strike it out with a diagonal line through the 4 square.*

◆ *Count/add on 2 more. Is 6 a multiple?*

Work through the 100 square striking out every one of the 2s. After you have crossed out a number ask the children to copy it on their 100 square. Each table has its own 'strike' (see below). This allows instant identification of those tables making a product.

Move onto 3s and repeat the procedure.

◆ *The 4s, 6s, 8s, 9s and 10s are all struck out as they are all multiples of 2s and 3s.*

Let the children move onto the 5s and 7s.

◆ *Which squares have not been struck out? These are the numbers which are not made by any other numbers. They are the 'prime' numbers Eratosthenes discovered.*

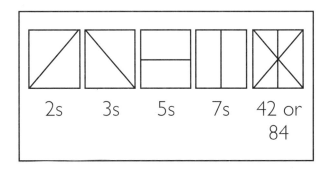

| 2s | 3s | 5s | 7s | 42 or 84 |

IDEAS FOR DISPLAY
Using a 100 number line attach yellow, pink, blue and steel (to represent grey) paper-clips to the different numbers. Leave unclipped the 'primes'. Allot various numbers to different groups, then on Friday look at the numbers to which they have attached the paper-clips. For example 30 will have yellow 15, pink 10 and blue 6.

EXTENSION WORK
Poster Puzzle: this can be carried out as a whole class mini-lesson using the 18 'm' tiles, a 'cm' tile. Gather the children around the multiplication grid poster. Show one of the 'm' for 'multiple' tiles.

◆ *Let's make a horizontal row of multiples for 7. (The children can help you put tiles across the grid.)*

◆ *Let's do the same for the 9s column. There is one point where the two intersect. What number is it? (63.) This number has a special name. It is a 'common multiple'.*

◆ *Common means 'shared alike'. Put the 'cm' tile on 63.*

Do a few more examples. On following days put a 'cm' tile on the grid and ask the class to plot the multiple paths to it.

DIVISION AND MULTIPLICATION

IS IT STILL THE SAME?

GROUP SIZE AND ORGANISATION
Whole class.
DURATION
30 minutes.
LEARNING OBJECTIVE
To revise multiplication sentences (and the words 'multiplicand', 'multiplier' and 'product').

YOU WILL NEED
Multiplication grid poster, blank tiles, card strips (see 'Let's look at the poster', page 15), chalkboard/flipchart.

WHAT TO DO
Pin up the multiplication grid poster. Choose a product or allow the children to pick one. Put a blank tile over it and ask the children which numbers make it. Two other children can hold up the card strips to highlight the multiplicand and the multiplier. Write an example on the board, for instance 7 × 8 can be 8 × 7. Whichever way round it is, the product remains the same. Write another example on the board, such as 4 × 9. Personalise it with a group of three children.
- ◆ *Who is the multiplicand?* (9) *Put your tile in its place.*
- ◆ *Who is the multiplier?* (4) *Put your tile in place.*
- ◆ *Now who is the product? Where will your tile go?*
Ask the class if the tiles could go in any other places. If 9 was identified as column 9 there is also row 9 so there are two positions for all table sentences, except which? Numbers multiplying themselves (2 × 2).

MAKE IT MATCH

GROUP SIZE AND ORGANISATION
Whole class then groups.
DURATION
60 minutes.
LEARNING OBJECTIVES
To make the link between division sentences and multiplication. To meet the new words 'dividend', 'divisor' and 'quotient'.

YOU WILL NEED
Paper strips $3\frac{1}{2}$ cm wide cut widthways from A4 paper,

multiplication grid poster, blank 4.5cm × 4.5cm paper tiles, chalkboard/flip chart, writing materials. For the extension work – three tiles lettered 'm', 'm' and 'p' and three lettered 'd', 'd' and 'q'.

WHAT TO DO
Gather the class around the poster. Choose a multiplication sentence and cover the numbers with the tiles. *What if we were asking not 4 × 9 = 36 but how many 9s in 36?* On the board write 36 ÷ 9=? *Would the tiles need to be changed?* Point out that 36 can be seen in the vertical 9 column where the 4s row joins it, so there are 4 nines in 36.

Write another example on the board such as 56 ÷7=? Ask the class to tell you which number to start with. They should say 56. Explain that this is called the *dividend*. Ask what it is divided by (7). This is the *divisor*. Next ask the children to show you where the dividend is and which divisor column it is in. Then ask them to show you the row that joins it. It is in the 8s row. This number is called the *quotient*. It tells us how many sets of divisors there are. Recap using different examples.

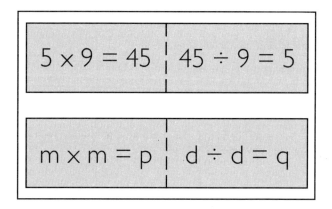

Organise the children into three groups A, B and C and demonstrate what you want them to do. Take one of the paper strips and fold it in half. Write a multiplication sentence such as 5 × 9 = 45 on one side. On the other side write a division story to match it: in this case 45 ÷ 9 = 5. Tell the groups to start with tables sentences. When they are confident with the activity ask them to think of matching pairs of number sentences within these limits: Group A to 100, B to 500 and C to 1000. In the plenary session, look at the pairs of number sentences the children have made.

IDEAS FOR DISPLAY
Use the children's strips as the basis of a display. They will need to copy one side of their sentences onto a fresh strip of paper.

FRACTIONS

Fractions represent 'unfinished' division calculations. Times tables can be expressed as fractions, showing another aspect of both the tables and division. The words 'numerator' and 'denominator' and the function of the fraction bar are explained.

DIVISION STORY

GROUP SIZE AND ORGANISATION
Whole class then individuals.
DURATION
45 minutes.
LEARNING OBJECTIVE
To see how the times tables can be compiled as fractions.

YOU WILL NEED
Multiplication grid poster, photocopiable page 23, blank tiles, Blu-Tack, chalkboard/flip chart, writing materials.

WHAT TO DO
Gather the children around the multiplication grid poster and tell them that together you are going to make a division story.
◆ *What number do we start with?* (Choose a number in the grid, such as 45, and place a blank tile over it.)
◆ *Now what are going to do with it?* (Divide it.) *Divide it by what? We have two choices, 5 or 9.* (Choose, say, 5

and put a tile over the 5 on the vertical column.)
◆ *So 45 divided by 5 equals how many?* (9. Put a tile over this number in the horizontal row.)
Next explain that you are going to show another way of dividing 45 using these same three numbers. Explain that because you are dividing you will use the numbers in the same order. Ask the class what the starting number was. Remove the tile and write 45 on the board.
◆ *What was it divided by?* (5)
◆ *Look carefully. I am not writing a division sign. I am writing a line underneath the 45 and putting 5 under that. This line is another way of saying 'shared by' or 'divided by'. What do you think comes next?* (Elicit the answer 'equals sign' from the children.) *And then ..? 9. So 45 fifths equals 9 wholes.*

Give each child a copy of photocopiable page 23. Go over the examples on the sheet to make sure the class have fully understood then let them complete the column $\frac{6}{2} =$, $\frac{9}{3} =$, and so on.

If children complete this row satisfactorily, allow them to fill in the rest of the sheet. If not, keep working together through the columns until most of the class are successful. Tell the children to write their names on the sheets and retain them for the next lesson.

FRACTION TRAINS

GROUP SIZE AND ORGANISATION
Individuals then groups.
DURATION
45 minutes.
LEARNING OBJECTIVE
To demonstrate understanding of fractions tables.

YOU WILL NEED
Children's completed (and correct) copies of photocopiable page 23 from the previous lesson, chalkboard/flip chart, long strips of paper, writing materials.

WHAT TO DO
Give the children back their photocopiable sheets from the previous session and discuss how fractions can be another way of expressing times tables, for example $4 = \frac{12}{3}$. Write it on the board. Encourage the children to look at the fractions tables on their photocopiable sheets to find other fractions that make 4 and draw up a train of them. For instance: $4 = \frac{12}{3} = \frac{28}{7} = \frac{36}{9} = \frac{16}{4} = \frac{24}{6}$

Work through another example and then assign the children into groups to write up their own on the long strips of paper: Group A should make a train three fractions long; Group B should make a train five fractions long; and Group C should make a train eight fractions long.

During the plenary session at the end of the activity, discuss the different groups' findings.

IDEAS FOR DISPLAY
Use the fraction trains as the basis for a display. Enlarged with marker pens on to strips of sugar paper they would make an excellent border for a maths board.

FRACTION SENTENCES

GROUP SIZE AND ORGANISATION
Whole class.
DURATION
30 minutes.
LEARNING OBJECTIVE
To learn about 'numerator', 'denominator' and 'whole number' in relation to fractions tables.

YOU WILL NEED
Blank tiles – 4.5cm × 4.5cm, one with = sign, one with fraction bar, marker pen, multiplication grid poster, Blu-Tack, chalkboard/flip chart.

WHAT TO DO
Tell the children that in this lesson the class will be making some fraction sentences together using the multiplication grid. Start with a number to be divided, for example 24. Using the Blu-Tack, stick a blank tile over it and write 24 on the tile.

Explain that this number has a special name. It is called the *numerator* and is the top number of a fraction. Ask the class what number could go underneath it. Refer to the grid, and elicit that it could be either 6 or 4 or 8 or 3. Choose one, say, 6. Explain that this number is the divisor and is called the *denominator*. Cover it with a blank tile and write 6 over it. Now ask the children what the answer to this would be. Hopefully they will be able to give you the answer 4. Explain that this is the *whole number*. Cover this number on the poster with a blank tile. When all three numbers are covered on the multiplication grid poster, re-create the fraction sentence on the board using the = sign and the fraction bar. When you have done this, make up some more examples with the class.

EXTENSION WORK
Poster puzzle: Tell the children you will be putting 'n', 'd' and 'wn' tiles on the grid every morning. Set the children a time by which you will have expected them to have worked out the fraction sentence.

FRACTIONS TABLES

Name _____   Date _____

COMMUTATIVE CALCULATOR

This demonstrates through a simple calculator that a × b = b × a = c. Different ways of writing multiplication sentences are explored.

ECONOMY STAIRCASE

GROUP SIZE AND ORGANISATION
Whole class then individuals.
DURATION
45 minutes.
LEARNING OBJECTIVE
To explore the commutative law of multiplication.

YOU WILL NEED
Photocopiable page 25 (only the top half is needed for this lesson, cut off and retain the bottom half for the next lesson), thin card, multiplication grid poster, blank tiles 4.5cm × 4.5cm, Blu-Tack.

WHAT TO DO
Before the lesson paste the top half of photocopiable page 25 on to card. Write the children's names on the reverse. Leave to dry, then cut out the two parts.

Gather the class around the poster. Using the blank tiles, revise how 3 × 4 has the same product as 4 × 3. Let the class do some more 'reverse' pairs. (You may like to blank out one half of the poster grid, showing how it is repeated diagonally in the other half.)

Give out the triangles you prepared earlier. Show how the corner can be moved on the 'economy staircase' with the black edges lining up rows and columns. The arrow points to the product. Pick two numbers, say 7 × 8. Line them up with the triangle. The class will see there is only one way of doing this.

◆ *What product do we get? Does it matter to the product if we say 7 multiplied by 8 or 8 multiplied by 7?*

When the children are confident, compare the staircase with the multiplication grid poster.
◆ *What is the difference between them? It is not just that there are no '1s' multipliers, there are fewer products.*
◆ *How many products on the grid? How many on the staircase?*

In the plenary session, recap the use of the triangle calculator. Emphasise that it means the children only have to learn half the times tables facts. They will know 7 × 8 and 8 × 7 have the same product. Retain the calculators for the next lesson.

COMMUTATION ALGEBRA

GROUP SIZE AND ORGANISATION
Whole class then individuals.
DURATION
45 minutes.
LEARNING OBJECTIVE
To demonstrate understanding of the commutative principles in multiplication, division and fractions formats by substituting numbers for letters in number sentence layouts.

YOU WILL NEED
One staircase calculator per child from the previous session, the bottom half of photocopiable page 25, writing materials.

WHAT TO DO
Give the children back their calculators and economy staircases and draw their attention to the equation on the triangular part of the calculator. One number ,'a', multiplied by another called 'b' equals another called 'c'.
◆ *What would we call 'c'? The product. Let's try it using a product.* (Choose one, such as 40.) *What could 'a' be?* 4.
◆ *So 'b' is?* 10. *What's the reverse of that?* 10 × 4.
Give the children the bottom half of photocopiable page 25. Point out how it shows different ways of writing multiplication and division sentences. The letters 'a', 'b' and 'c' have been used for multiplication and division. Tell the children to use their staircase to pick five different table sentences and their reverses.

Finally, do the children see how some products are shown twice on the staircase. What are these and why do they appear twice? (12, 16, 18, 20, 24, 30, 36, 40 are products which are in more than two tables.)

RESOURCE BANK

MULTIPLICATION AND DIVISION FACTS

ECONOMY STAIRCASE

Name _____   Date _____

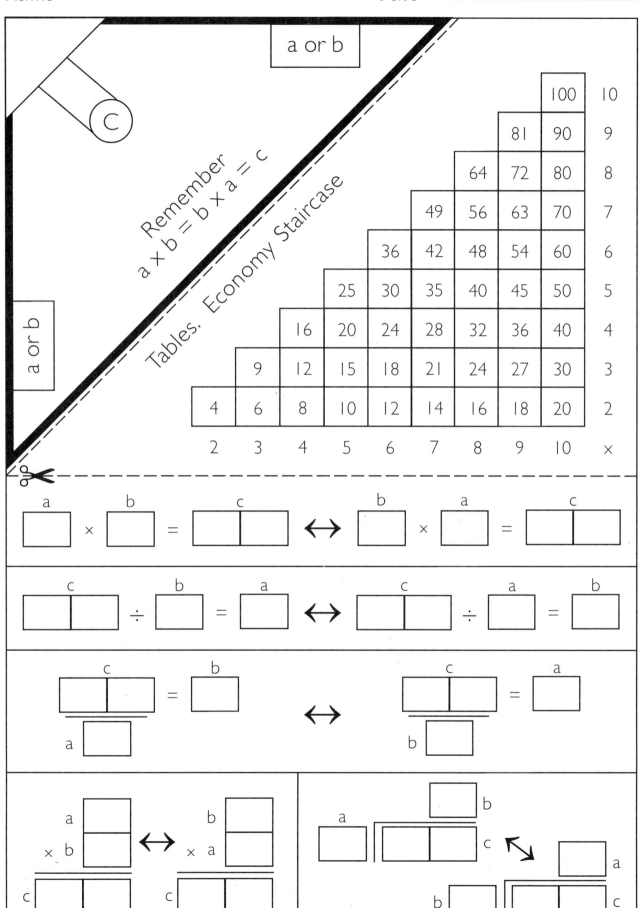

a or b

© C

Remember
a × b = b × a = c

Tables. Economy Staircase

×	2	3	4	5	6	7	8	9	10	
10									100	
9								81	90	
8							64	72	80	
7						49	56	63	70	
6					36	42	48	54	60	
5				25	30	35	40	45	50	
4			16	20	24	28	32	36	40	
3		9	12	15	18	21	24	27	30	
2	4	6	8	10	12	14	16	18	20	

FIND THE FACTORS

GROUP SIZE AND ORGANISATION
Whole class, then individuals.
DURATION
60 minutes.
LEARNING OBJECTIVE
To learn what a factor is and to make factor tables.

YOU WILL NEED
Photocopiable page 27, paper slips 14cm × 5cm one per child, multiplication grid poster, writing and drawing materials, scissors, stapler.

WHAT TO DO
Hand out the copies of photocopiable page 27. Tell the children to look at the first factors table. Explain that it shows a square for the product – the number in the centre; so 4 is made by 2 and 2; 6 is made by 3 and 2, and so on. Ask them to complete the 2s table. Check that the children understand what they are doing then ask them to complete the rest of the photocopiable sheet. As the children finish, let them make a book cover using the paper strip. When a correct column is completed, the children can cut the table out and staple or paste it to the paper strip. The children can colour the factors in the family colour code. The right-hand side of the column will be in the family colour code, the other side will be in a variety of colours. The product should be left uncoloured.

MULTIPLE FACTORS

GROUP SIZE AND ORGANISATION
Whole class then groups.
DURATION
45 minutes.
LEARNING OBJECTIVE
To search the grid for products and categorise them into two factor and multi-factor products.

YOU WILL NEED
Paper, scissors, children's factor table books from the previous session, economy staircases, multiplication grid poster, writing and drawing materials.

WHAT TO DO
Gather the children around the multiplication grid poster. They will see that some products are on it more than once. Ask them to find some. Inevitably someone will give the example of the 1 × ? product. Explain that 1 cannot be a factor as it is not multiplying anything. It just states the obvious: there is one whatever. As other examples are given, tell the class to check them in their factor books and/or on the economy staircase. Some products, such as 24 and 40, are shown more than once even on the economy staircase. These are multi-factor products.

Tell the children that you want them to find all the products with two factors and all those with four or more. The products with two factors will be shown as bow ties. The product will be the knot in the middle and the two factors will be the bows on either side.

Those products which have more than two factors will be shown as flowers. The product will be in the centre and the factors will be the petals with the factor pairs opposite each other. Divide the class into three groups and split the factors between them: Group A factors 2, 3, 10; Group B factors 4, 5, 6; and Group C factors 7, 8, 9.

When the children have completed their bow-ties and flowers they should colour them in using the colour family code. (Refer to the times tables poster.) When they are finished, tell the children to cut them out. Discuss the outcomes in the plenary session. Ask

the class which products have only two factors which are the same (9, 25, 49, 81). Groups can display their drawings and the correct ones can be put on display.

IDEAS FOR DISPLAY
Use coloured paper in the corresponding times tables code to make enlarged bow ties and flowers. Write the factors on them with a marker pen.

EXTENSION WORK
Poster Puzzle: tell the children that every morning you will be putting one 'f' and one 'p' tile on the poster. Their job is to find the 'f' tile's partner.

FACTOR TABLES

Name _____   Date _____

2	4	2
3	6	2
4	8	2
5		2
6		2
7		2
8		2
9		2

2	6	3
3		
4		
5		
6		
7		
8		
9		

2	8	4

2	10	5

2		6

2		7

2		8

2		9

MULTIPLICATION AND DIVISION FACTS

PHOTOCOPIABLE
RESOURCE
BANK

Products are split diagrammatically – initially into factors and thence into prime factors. Notation is introduced as preparation for work with indices.

FACTOR FOREST

GROUP SIZE AND ORGANISATION
Whole class then individuals.
DURATION
45 minutes.
LEARNING OBJECTIVE
To learn to factorize numbers diagrammatically as a two branch factor tree.

YOU WILL NEED
Paper, writing and drawing materials, multiplication grid poster.

WHAT TO DO
Choose a product from the grid, such as 45.
◆ *What are its factors?* (The top is 9 and the side is 5 or vice versa) *So 5 and 9 work together to make 45.* Explain that you are going to show the children how to draw a factor tree. This will be another way of showing factors.
◆ *45 is the trunk of the tree. The trunk branches out in two directions. Here one branch is 5 and the other is 9.* Work through some more examples of this type.

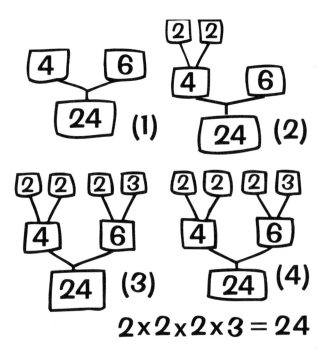

$$2 \times 2 \times 2 \times 3 = 24$$

Then let the children make some factor trees. To begin with set them the number 28. Go round the class and check that everyone is working satisfactorily. Once they have grasped the idea let them create their own 'trees'. The factors can be coloured in the tables colour code. Work through the children's examples in the plenary session.

IDEAS FOR DISPLAY
Display the different factor trees as a factor forest.

PRIME FACTORS

GROUP SIZE AND ORGANISATION
Whole class or group.
DURATION
30 minutes.
LEARNING OBJECTIVE
To find prime factors and write them as number sentences.

YOU WILL NEED
Paper, writing materials, chalkboard/flip chart, chalk or marker pens in the appropriate colour code.

WHAT TO DO
Explain that in this lesson you want the children to make two branch factor trees. For example 24 will become 4 × 6.
◆ *Are any of the factors multiples of any other numbers? Yes, 4 is two 2s. So we could do two more branches for 4.*
◆ *What about 6? It is two 3s. It can have two branches.* Colour all the 'leaves' in the corresponding times tables poster colour code, thereby showing the transformations of tables into the basic four tables.
◆ *So we have 2 × 2 × 2 × 3 making 24. What are 2 and 3? They are prime numbers. So 2 × 2 × 2 × 3 are the prime factors of 24. Let's write this number sentence underneath.*
Set the children the task of creating number trees for 16 and 63. As the children encounter 63 they will realise that 7 is a stopping point. They may feel their trees look lopsided but reassure them that this is correct. Tell the children to try 90, 72 and then let them make up their own numbers.
Go over what the children have done for 90 and 72 in the plenary session.

POWERS AND LOWEST COMMON MULTIPLES

Powers of numbers are introduced as a method of shorthand notation, while searching for the lowest common multiple of two numbers under 100 is introduced as a demonstration of the usefulness of prime factors and powers.

POWER TRAINS

GROUP SIZE AND ORGANISATION
Whole class then individuals.
DURATION
50 minutes.
LEARNING OBJECTIVE
To learn about powers and index notation.

YOU WILL NEED
Photocopiable page 31, (cut the 'trains' into two strips, save the bottom halves for the lowest common multiples), writing materials, blank paper strips.

WHAT TO DO
Remind the children that when they made factor 'trees', they ended up with prime factors which were sometimes multiplied by themselves one after another, for example, $24 = 2 \times 2 \times 2 \times 3$. Explain that today they are going to see how this long train of 2s can be written in a shorter way.

Hand out Strip A to each child and organise the class into the three basic groups. Assign each group to a particular factor, for instance Group A could use 2s, Group B 3s and Group C 5s.

Tell the children to look at strip A on their sheet. Do they see that the number boxes are like a train of three wagons with the engine at the back? Tell the groups to fill their boxes with their group factor. Then ask them to read them out, for example $2 \times 2 \times 2$.

◆ *How many times have your factors multiplied themselves?* 3
◆ *Let's look at the other side of the sentence. We have a number box.*
◆ *What number will it hold do you think? Do you think it holds the product?* (8, 27, 125)
◆ *But that is not another way of writing $2 \times 2 \times 2$ and what is the smaller box above the number box?*
◆ *It holds the number which shows how many times the main number multiplies itself, so what number do you think should go in it?* 3
◆ *When we do this we say a number has been multiplied 'to the power of'. In this case it is multiplied to the power of 3. The two boxes are a short way of showing the 'power' of a number, rather like an engine is the power of a train. Write the power of your factor in the small box.*

Tell the children to look at the second number sentence. How is it different? This time there are seven boxes and the 'power engine' is at the front. Working in their groups, explain that you want some to use four boxes, some five boxes, some six boxes and some of them all seven boxes to make different number trains.

Move on to Strip B. Ask the children to fill it in using any two prime factors. These can be multiplied together in any combination to 10. (See Figure 4.) Next try the reverse order with factors and powers first. Use different factors and different combinations.

COMMON MULTIPLES

GROUP SIZE AND ORGANISATION
Class/group
DURATION
Two sessions of 45 minutes.
LEARNING OBJECTIVES
To revise common multiples first introduced in Multiples and Primes and learn how indices and prime factors can be employed together to find the lowest common multiple.

YOU WILL NEED
Multiplication grid poster, blank tiles, Blu-Tack, the bottom halves of photocopiable page 31, writing materials.

POWERS AND LOWEST COMMON MULTIPLES

WHAT TO DO

Session one: Remind the children that when they learned about multiples they found a common multiple for two table numbers (see 'Extension work' on page 19). They made 'paths' of multiples of a table leading to the common multiple. Can the class remember how they did it?

◆ *Let's find a common multiple for 8 and 6. Can a group of you make a path of multiples for the 8 across the grid?*

◆ *Now another group will make a path down for 6. When the 6s intersect with the 8s, the group can stop. Take away all those tiles in the 8s column that have gone past the intersection square.*

◆ *Let's see what number is under this tile. It is 48. So 48 is a common multiple for 8 and 6. But is it the first, the lowest common multiple, there is? Let's peel off the tiles one by one and see if we can find any other multiples that are the same for the two tables.*

Peel off the blank tiles to 16 for 8s and 24 for 6s. The children should recognise 24 is a multiple of both. Peel back the rest of the tiles.

◆ *So we can see 24 is also a common multiple of 8 and 6. If we were looking for other numbers, would this be the easiest way to do it? Can you carry the poster and the tiles around with you? What if the numbers were bigger than 100? We need a method for doing this. That is what we are going to learn next.*

Session Two: Remind the children about the time they made factor trees. What did they do? They split numbers into prime factors and wrote them in a type of number train (see 'Power trains' on page 29). Tell them that they are going to do both these things to find the lowest common multiple of two numbers.

Give out the bottom halves of photocopiable page 31. Start with 12 and 16 as an example . Write 12 in the left-hand rectangular box and 16 in the right-hand one. (See Figure 4.) Begin with the factors of 12. Look at the photocopiable sheet and explain that this tree hasn't got branches, they are more like roots. However, they still work the same way. 12 is 3 × 4. Write 3 and 4 in the two smaller boxes underneath. Ask the children if any number can be split up further? They should say 4 can become 2 × 2. Write these in the boxes underneath the 4. That is the end of the 'roots'.

Move down to the row marked * and write in the prime factors: 3 × 2 × 2. On the line underneath write them down as powers. (Although there may be too many boxes in this example, more complex numbers will need the extra space.)

Now move over to 16. When carrying out this example, use 2 × 8 so that the subdivisions reach the third line. You should have 2^4 . (See Figure 4.)

To find the lowest common multiple, pick out the highest prime factors of the two numbers from the double arrow row. As you cannot use the same prime factor twice you will end up with $3 × 2^4$.

Using a calculator, multiply the prime factors $3 × 2^4$. Fill in the bottom row. In this example the lcm = 48.

In their groups ask children to try further examples: Group A use numbers up to 20; Group B numbers between 20 and 50; and Group C numbers over 50.

Figure 4

RESOURCE BANK

MULTIPLICATION AND DIVISION FACTS

POWER TRAINS

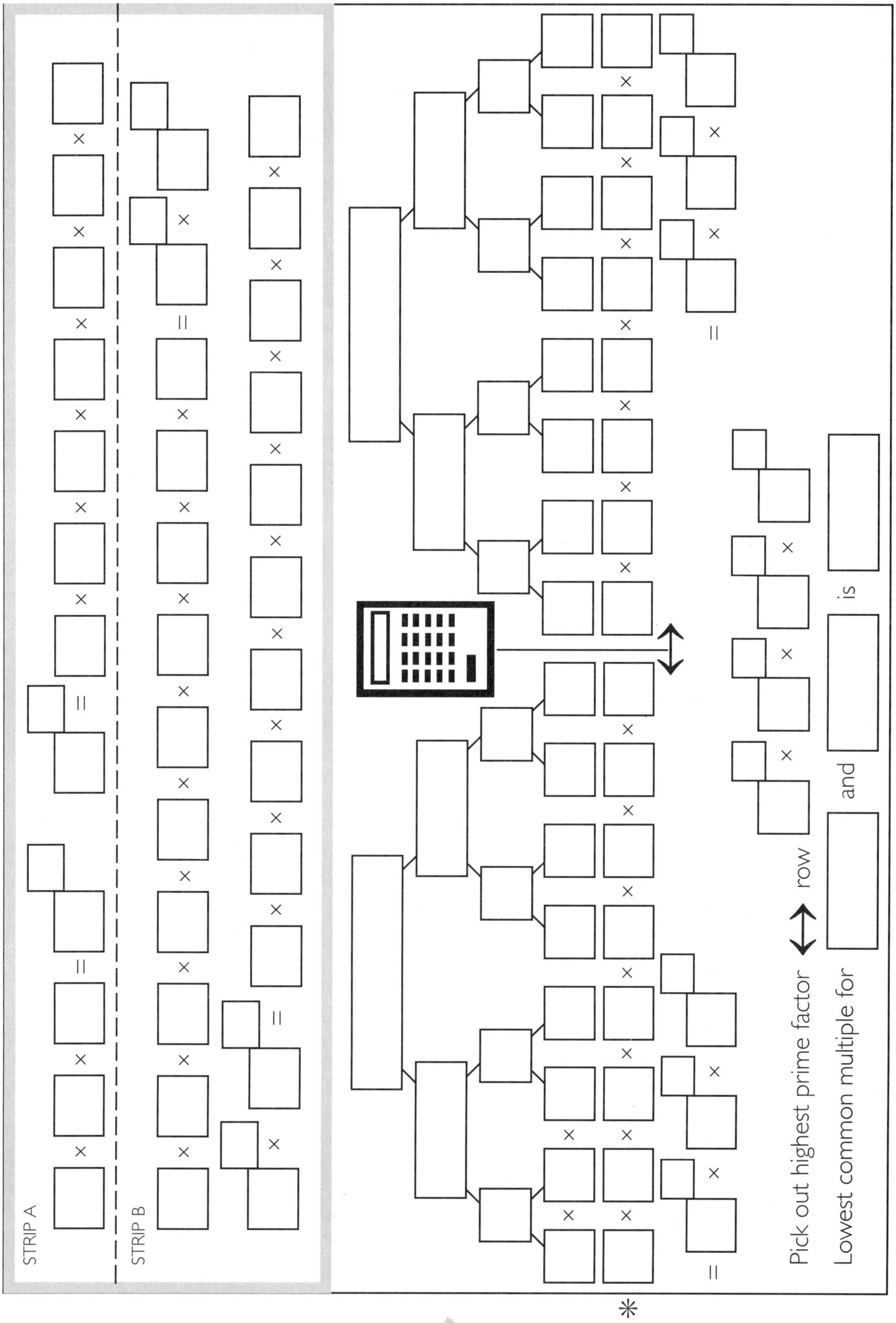

STRIP A

STRIP B

Pick out highest prime factor ↔ row

Lowest common multiple for [ ] and [ ] is [ ]

＊

SUMMING UP

GROUP SIZE AND ORGANISATION
Whole class
DURATION
45 minutes.
LEARNING OBJECTIVE
To revise the multiplication facts and new number properties introduced.

YOU WILL NEED
Blank tiles, poster, product cards made by enlarging photocopiable page 18 to A3, pasting it onto card and leaving it to dry (when dry cut out the grid cards only and put them in an opaque bag), Blu-Tack.

WHAT TO DO
This is a fun game in which the multiplication grid poster is used to reinforce the various activites the children have carried out. The aim of the game will vary according to the revision you want to do. It centres around any three numbers of a times table sentence, for example 'Eight 3s make 24, how many 8s

in 24', or terminology in groups of three such as multiplicand, multiplier, product; dividend, divisor, quotient; numerator, denominator, whole number; a, b, c; factor, factor, product.

Choose your objective and split the class into groups of three. Shake the bag and draw out a card. Ask the first group to complete the table sentence or to identify the numbers with words. For example if 18 is drawn out, the trio have to state $3 \times 6 = 18$ or $18 \div 6 = 3$ or if 56 is the dividend and the divisor is 6, the quotient is 3.

If the children get it right, they put a blank tile over the 18 square on the grid poster. Do not replace the card in the bag as cards can only be used once. If the answer is incorrect, the question is thrown open to the whole class. Allow the first child who gives the correct answer to put a tile on the product square. Go round the class in turn. The first trio to put a tile in place making a line of three across, down or diagonally or completing a square of four are the winners.

ASSESSMENT
The children's responses to the game give you the opportunity to assess the class's strengths and weaknesses.